Poems from the Rising Sun

Special Edition

© Alta H Haffner 2024
ALL RIGHTS RESERVED
ISBN:9780796180261

www.sakurabookpublishing.com

Katherine E Winnick (Brighton-UK)

Andy N (Manchester-UK)

Janet Scarborough (USA)

Alta H Haffner (South Africa)

Charles R Haffner (USA)

RJ Tungsten (USA)

tranquil and peaceful
a river of memories
heaven reflected

Alta H Haffner

the morning moon
wanes with rising sun
we meet

Katherine E Winnick

Glimmering stars
filling up the night sky
delivers hope slowly

Charles R Haffner

summer's threatening clouds
flowers begging for their drink
rain sizzled asphalt

RJ Jungsten

Daily disbelief
one day you see bright sunshine
then you see the rain

Andy N

Orange flowers bloom
Wind blows through the large oak trees
Pink sky of late eve

Janet Scarborough

butterflies hover
waltzing with empathy
the crow flies

Katherine E Winnick

Many blinking lights
surround a mountain lake
fireflies congregate

Charles R Haffner

lanterns burning bright
breathtaking Hirosaki
Sakura backdrop

Alta H Haffner

daytime scorching heat
like a former lover's touch
during night's passion

RJ Jungsten

Crows sleeping on branches
Moonlight dodging falling leaves
a whisper escapes

Charles R Haffner

she circled the words
etched deep upon her soul
in violet ink

Katherine E Winnick

Golden scales gleam
in a quiet mountain stream
one bear fishing

Charles R. Haffner

Autumn is coming
the trees wave goodbye
to the sunshine

Andy N

boats rowing slowly
fishing under the moonlight
crickets sing til dawn

Alta H Haffner

Morning sun rays
creating a pink glow,
before winds take
the sweet cherry scent
away this afternoon

Charles R Haffner

heart skipping a beat
internal compass spinning
direction unknown

RJ Tungsten

Each morning you can
hear the crunches of footsteps
making their way
from the front door to mailbox
covered in inches of snow

Charles R Haffner

a crimson dusk
hidden without a trace
kissed by the moonlight

Katherine E Winnick

Jumping home to home
causing little ripples
run nomad frog

Charles R Haffner

pen strokes decorate
the blank canvas of paper
our eyes tell the tale

RJ Jungsten

Heavy rain on windows
rattles as the wind picks up
changing both our moods

Andy N

Horse runs through the field
The sweet scent of daffodils
Bright yellow sun gleams

Janet Scarborough

meadows of blossoms
the beauty of tiny buds
Hanami at dawn

Alta H Haffner

Little trails follow
dancers on their icy floors
sharing everything

Charles R Haffner

beautiful autumn
rusty leaves falling slowly
soak up life's moments

Alta H Haffner

movement caught by sight
instinct overtakes the mind
body lead by soul

RJ Jungsten

Frozen flowers
precious moments displayed
on golden canvas

Charles R Haffner

cerise petals
dripping droplets of love
pure delight

Katherine E Winnick

running for a dream
legs moving on emotion
heart commands the brain

RJ Tungsten

Blown over the road
Leaves display a short cut home
when it starts to rain

Andy N

Colors still hiding
under blankets of late snow
winter's final fight

Charles R Haffner

Raining on your roof
you are both missing summer
before you get home

Andy N

Pink petals scattering
across the orchard in
the morning breeze.
Butterflies bring offerings
to share mother nature's love

Charles R Haffner

growth isn't finite
physically or mentally
extra room for all

RJ Jungsten

Washed out holiday
Next year you will go away
a month earlier

Andy N

moon's glow reflected
the glistening pavement below
concrete made mirror

RJ Tungsten

Branches conceal our path
as our muddy road leads us
home, fueled by the tears

Charles R Haffner

Steps into the woods
the branches blocks out the sun
farewell to summer

Andy N

Skies of sapphire
bizarre and ostentatious
when you fall you fly

Katherine E Winnick

Tree line canopy
nature's organic tunnel
sunglasses removed

RJ Jungsten

Tired eyes struggle
focusing on love's real truth
clearness between blinks

RJ Tungsten

Moonlit covered path
distant temple bell echoes
gifts to behold now

Alta H Haffner

Two dogs at sunset
keep barking in the river
don't want to come out

Andy N

vibrant cardinal perched
remembrance for those who've past
flowing tears of joy

RJ Jungsten

glistening sunrise
white mountain snow horizen
melted memories

Alta H Haffner

Blanket of fresh snow
Red birds chirping overhead
The first light of morn

Janet Scarborough

lost in the distance
salt water marsh captivates
unending beauty

RJ Tungsten

enchanted temple
cold frosted emerald path
sitting Buddha greets

Alta H Haffner

condensation drips
from the morning rain, voices
fill the coffee shop
new ideas and relations
formed with caffeine and pastries

RJ Tungsten

the star collapses
turning in on itself
like magic

Katherine E Winnick

scarlet petals fall
muddy ground covered with gifts
nature's earth nourished

Alta H Haffner

scoping out bookshelves
sneak peak into another's
play-land of the mind

RJ Jungsten

ancient syllables
the language of peace
our tranquility

Alta H Haffner

inner light obscured
nature's fury on display
rising up against
storms destroying vivid dreams
winds create broken pieces

RJ Jungsten

Silver dove gray sky
Cedar trees of powdered white
Soft dusty sunlight

Janet Scarborough

blossoming ideals
echoing halls of existence
etched in time

Katherine E Winnick

skies of amber dusk
halfmoon hiding between clouds
stars greeting lovers

Alta H Haffner

lips tracing your nape
hips sway like a rocking boat
when two become one

RJ Tungsten

cactus sun salute
standing tall in heat or cold
desert protector

RJ Tungsten

piercing cold forest
whispering winds dance through trees
bright flickering stars

Janet Scarborough

summer rainfall dawn
glowing colorful rainbow
traces across my heart

Alta H Haffner

ecstasy of touch
love spoken by fingertips
exhilarating

RJ Jungsten

bright morning sunrise
butterflies feast on petals
sipping black coffee

I wake up to see beauty
fall asleep with memories

Alta H Haffner

wish granted
random synchronicity
fragments of time

Katherine E Winnick

snowflakes falling down
trees under starry night sky
the sound of silence

Janet Scarborough

disheveled child
cold fingers work his zipper
School bus, don' t run late

RJ Jungsten

dark storm clouds floating
an old well granting wishes
as the fireflies dance

Alta H Haffner

Entering Autumn
the woods know they will see you less
the colder it gets

Andy N

wonderful sparkles
icy tree branches glisten
golden light of morn

Janet Scarborough

scarlet strands
rain kissed blossoms
conquer the waters

Katherine E Winnick

with each labored breath
I'm succumbing to your Grace
rising to meet you

RJ Jungsten

the break of sunrise
romantic Sakura path
blossoms blossoming

Alta H Haffner

Blue sky early dawn
post summer you wonder how
it will follow you

Andy N

tight walking the edge
where danger and life embrace
life blurring the line

RJ Jungsten

sweet raindrops
these delicate wings
fluttering gently

Katherine E Winnick

no perspective like
a near death experience
to keep things in check

RJ Jungsten

foggy dusky night
waves crash into onyx rocks
icy rain shimmers

Janet Scarborough

endless energy
my soul breathes in the sun rays
absorbing new life

RJ Jungsten

awakening love
gratitude surrounding now
moonlight greets dawns light

Alta H Haffner

black frigid nightfall
symphony of soulful waves
shining silver moon

Janet Scarborough

dance and mesmerize
flames as they swallow kindling
gorgeous destruction

RJ Tungsten

forbidden paths
tuning into my soul
a matter of chance

Katherine E Winnick

glossy snow crystals
silent enchanted forest
red cardinal sings

Janet Scarborough

journey of struggling
life's masts are meant to be climbed
keep moving aloft

RJ Jungsten

intricate petals
bursting fusion of thoughts
colors of skin

Katherine E Winnick

matcha moonlight drink
as the stars glistens brightly
love forevermore

Alta H Haffner

www.ingramcontent.com/pod-product-compliance
Lightning Source LLC
Chambersburg PA
CBHW042043290426
44109CB00001B/19